To Frank

Thanks

Nothing More, Nothing Less, Just Me 2

'The Casanova Edition'

Jason O'Neal Williams
'Prince Jason'
The Prince of Poetry

Prince Jason

Sept. 1, 2010

Nothing More, Nothing Less, Just Me 2

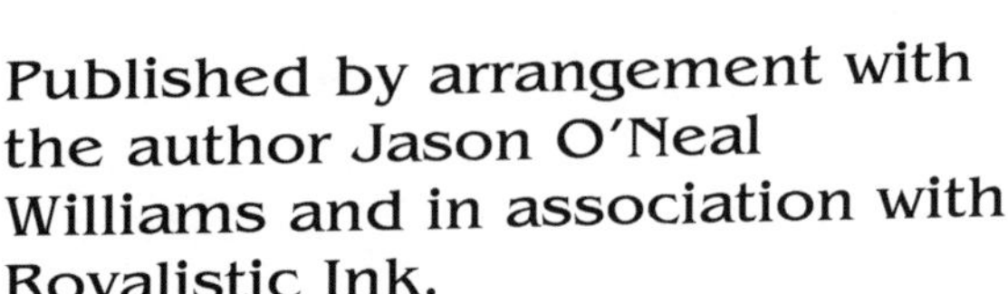

A Royalistic Ink Book

Published by arrangement with the author Jason O'Neal Williams and in association with Royalistic Ink.

Brandon Jenkins

- **Experience**

Illustrating, pencils, inking and painting

Editor

Jason O'Neal Williams
"Prince Jason"
The Prince of Poetry and Storytelling

- 2002 International Poet of the Year nominee
- 2002 International Poet Merit Award
- 2002 Editor's Choice Award
- 2003 Appearance in Ebony magazine
- 2004 Pinkie Carolyn Wilkerson Award for Literacy and Poetry-Presented to him by Grambling State University
- 2004 International Who's Who In Poetry-The only American featured poet for that year

- 2006 Pinkie Carolyn Wilkerson Award for Literacy and Poetry- Presented to him by Grambling State University

Websites

www.authorsden.com/princejason

www.authorsden.com/jb3

www.myspace.com/prince_jason

Email address

majortalent2003@yahoo.com
onealwill@yahoo.com

Expression

First given honor to God. I can do all things through Jesus who strengthens me.

Prince Jason

About The Author

Jason O'Neal Williams, also known as Prince Jason "The Prince of Poetry and Storytelling" was born July 21, 1978 in Houston Texas. His education is in Marketing and Literature to which he studied at Grambling State University, he graduates in 2002. He is a Poet, Author, Professional Writer Speaker, Editor, Columnist, Literary Agent, Screenwriter, Actor and CEO of Royalistic Ink.

He has appeared in Ebony Magazine in 2003 and was a poetry writer for Black College Today Magazine. Jason has been awarded the 2004 Pinkie Carolyn Wilkerson Award - Literacy and Poetry, Grambling State, 2006 Pinkie Carolyn Wilkerson Award - Literacy and Poetry, Grambling State 2004 International Who's Who In Poetry nominee-The only American featured poet for that year, 2002 International Poet of the year nominee, 2002 International Poet of Merit award, January 2002 Editor's choice award.

He has published poem "I Want To Succeed" in poetry anthology, "Solitude" (2002), Published poem "Rain" in poetry anthology, "New Millennium Poets" (2002), Published poem "We Are Poets" in poetry anthology, "International Who's Who In Poetry" (2004).

Jason's Books are:

- ✓ 1st Book: **"My Story, Through My Eyes"** (2003) Publish America
- ✓ 2nd Book: **"E.3"** (**E**xperiencing Death, **E**motional Disturbance, **E**verlasting Love) 2004- Publish America
- ✓ 3rd book **The Life That I Live** (2005) Publish America
- ✓ 4th book **I Must Confess, "The Lost Pages"** (2005) Publish America

- ✓ 5th book, **2 Sides To A Story** (2005) Publish America

- ✓ 6th book **Prince Jason, Welcome to my Kingdom** (2007) Starving Writers Publishing
- ✓ 7th book **7** (2008) Starving Writers Publishing/Royalistic Ink

- ✓ 8th **J.B.3** (2008) Royalistic Ink

- ✓ 9th book, **J.B.3 Coloring Book** (2008) Royalistic Ink

- ✓ 10th book, **Will I Make It To Heaven?** (2008) Royalistic Ink

- ✓ 11th book, **Evolution "Volume 1"** (2009) Royalistic Ink

- ✓ 12th book, **Evolution "Volume 2"** (2009) Royalistic Ink

- ✓ 13th book, **Love, Sex and Everything Else "Volume 1"** (2009) Royalistic Ink

- ✓ 14th book **Love, Sex and Everything Else "Volume 2"** (2009) Royalistic Ink

- ✓ 15th book **7 "2nd Edition"** (July 21, 2009) Royalistic Ink
- ✓ 16th book, **Nothing More, Nothing Less, Just Me** (July 21, 2009) Royalistic Ink

- ✓ 17th book, **J.B.3 Activate** (November 2009) Royalistic Ink

- ✓ 18th book, **Poetic Voices**, (December 2009) Royalistic Ink

- ✓ 19th book, **My Life is a Journey** (December 2009) Royalistic Ink

- ✓ 20th book, **The Poetry Prince** (December 2009) Royalistic Ink

- ✓ 21st book, **Nothing More, Nothing Less, Just Me 2 "The Casanova Edition"** (Feb. 2010) Royalistic Ink

Table of Contents

First Lady

Not number 2
Not number 3
Marry me
Be my first lady

First lady
I want you to be
Lets love each other
Unconditionally

First lady
Number one
Whenever we're together
We always have fun

First lady
Seductive, sexy
Your kisses
Fills me with ecstasy

I need the love that changes
me
The love I'm always giving
Charge my heart
So I can start living

The love in my heart
Flows rapidly
Being with you
Makes me so happy

Bliss
You give me a good reaction
Total glee affection
Plenty satisfaction

First time I saw you
I said, She's the one for me
I knew at that moment
You were my destiny

First lady
I love you so
When I propose to you
Please don't say no

Yes
I pray for this reply
I'm glad we met
I'm glad I said hi

Not number 2
Not number 3
Marry me
Be my first lady

So Fine

She got her own
She don't want mine
She's sexy
So fine

So fine
Walking her walk
So fine
Talking her talk

So fine
Elegance
Seductive perfume
Intelligence

So fine
Beautiful smile
Her phone number
I love to dial

So fine
Naturally pretty
I like her a lot
Really

Right now I'm acting silly
Just like an excited kid
It's all because of the things
you done and did

The way you are

The way you look
Very appealing
I love the way you look
The way you feel
My desire for you
I can't conceal

She got her own
She don't want mine
She's sexy
So fine

Sunshine

So beautiful
So fine
Will you be mine?
I need your sunshine

My girl
I love you so
Shine on me
With that special glow

No cloudy days
The sky is clear
The forecast is sunny
For the rest of the year

Sunshine
I'm warm when you're near
Your presence
Takes away my fear

Sunshine
A lovely vision I see
Your glow
Spread it all over me

I want to feel your pleasure
And experience some glee
Whenever I wake
It's you I want to see

When you smile

My frown leave
You're breath taking
It's hard to breathe
You take my air away
Overwhelming
Your essence lights up my day

Sunshine
I crave your embrace
Stay with me
Don't leave my place

Without you
I'm cold and lonely
You are my one and only

Just like the Temptations
What can make me feel this
way
I got sunshine
On a cloudy day

So beautiful
So fine
Will you be mine?
I need your sunshine

P.Y.T

TLC is what you give me
You make me feel good
constantly
P.Y.T

P.Y.T
Can I be with you?
Please say yes
I really like you
Two
Lets be together
Can I love you forever?

You control my heartbeat
It moves when you're near me
Your presence is what I require
Please stay near me
Don't stray
I need you everyday

P.Y.T
So pretty I see
I believe
We are meant to be

P.Y.T
The one I adore
I don't need less of you
I want more

P.Y.T

Pretty Young Thing
You make my soul sing
You make my heart dance
Take a risk
Give me a chance

P.Y.T
Pretty girl
Your smile
Lit up my whole world

TLC is what you give me
You make me feel good
constantly
P.Y.T

Thanks Again

Baby, honey
All the above
Thanks again
For showing me how to love

Your grace
Your sex appeal
You are my favorite meal

You're that good
Great to me
I was so nervous
When I ask for that 1st date with me

You didn't reject
You said yes
The best evening ever
Confess
Telling you what's true
Just like that old saying, I really dig you

Baby, honey
All the above
Thanks again
For showing me how to love

Nobody Else

I'm better because of you
Improved myself
All I need is you
Nobody else

I can stare into your eyes
forever
I can hold you longer
Your tender kiss
Makes me stronger

I can do everything
With you by my side
I can't live without you
I tried
But it didn't work out
Right now you're all I care
about

Whenever I write a love poem
You always come to my mind
A picture of perfection
So caring and kind
Sweet, elegant
I swear
You must be heaven sent

I'm better because of you
Improved myself
All I need is you
Nobody else

Hey Friend

This is just some stuff
I wanted to say
Hello friend
Hey

This poem is about my
observation
Hey friend
This is how we start our
conversation

Hey friend
This is how we greet
Hey friend
We say this whenever we meet

Unique style
Bashful presence
Inviting smile
Sweet essence

Cute
You're easygoing too
These are some of the things
I notice about you

It's just something about you
That I can't avoid or ignore
Maybe later on you can tell me
about your interests or hobbies

Because I really would like to
know more

This is just some stuff
I wanted to say
Hello friend
Hey

Ms. Sag is her Name

From your personality to your
appearance
I like them both the same
Ms. Sag is her name

The 1st day I met you
It was like a breath of fresh air
I was curious
Why does this young lady have
gray in her hair?

At first I was infatuated by your
body
Now I'm more impressed with
your mind
I am also overwhelmed by your
heart
It's good and kind

Hard to find
A woman like you is rare
Someone with compassion
And know how to care

Aware
I know I have a good friend
Whatever connection we have
is everlasting
It won't end

Contagious laugh

A smile I can't forget
You have pretty eyes
It's like watching a sunset

I can go on for days, weeks
Months and even a year
You told me write from my
heart
So I wrote this poem sincere

From your personality to your
appearance
I like them both the same
Ms. Sag is her name

Peach

Lessons she taught me
Teach
I will never forget
Peach

One day I met a girl
I called her Peach
She broke down my defense
Breach
Entered my heart
Fell in love with her
The very start

She was from Georgia
ATL
We knew each other
Very well

She said whenever I see you
I want to kiss you
I said whenever I'm not with
you
I miss you

So beautiful
She was to me
So pretty
So lovely

Every time our hands touched
Electricity felt

Every time her lips touched my
lips
My heart melt

She had an affect on me
No other woman had
She knew how to cheer me up
When I was sad or mad

Peach
I love saying her name
So much in common
She and I was the same

She was caring
She was smart
I was young and dumb
That's why we are apart

Lessons she taught me
Teach
I will never forget
Peach

Short and Sweet

I'm glad we had the chance to
meet
She was Short and Sweet

Cute
Long hair
Sexy body
Stare
Admire
She set my heart on fire
Acquire
I want her
Fixation
I really like her

I love to see your smile
I love to hear your laugh
Addition
Math
Not subtract
I like your personality
The way you act

React
Reaction
You fulfill me
Plenty of satisfaction

I think about you
All the time
I think about you

Every time I write a love rhyme

Reciting a special poem
So you can hear my care for
you
I want you to know
I will always be there for you

I'm glad we had the chance to
meet
She was Short and Sweet

Only You

Always and forever
Being true
I don't want anyone else
Only you

When you smile I see a piece of heaven
You have an angel face
So much comfort being with you
A peaceful place
Serenity
You really bring out the best in me

You're so sexy
Friendly and fun
There's more love to come
We've just begun

I adore you
More than you ever know
Right now we're getting to understand each other better
Taking things slow

This chance I won't blow
Taking my time
Girl you're a ten
You're a dime

I'm using this rhyme
To get you attention
Because baby
You have my full attention

I have some pension
But you don't want that from
me
She told me to treat her right
And also be honest with me

I agree
I told her, I will
She placed her hand on my
heart
And gave it a thrill

Always and forever
Being true
I don't want anyone else
Only you

I Want To Know What Love Is

It comes
And it go
What is love?
I want to know

Love has more than one
definition
When you ask a lady to marry
you
You ask for her permission

Condition
I'm trying to improve yours and
mine
Be my 1st lady
You're so fine

Ain't too proud to beg
I've told you this
I need your sweet kisses
I crave your sexual bliss

I want you to know what love is
Inform me
Show me something
I don't see

Let me feel something
Never felt before
You are someone
I will always adore

True love
It's hard to find
I'm speaking truthfully when I
say
You're always on my mind

Love is sharing and caring
Love is emotional
Love is an amazing feeling
Love is powerful

It comes
And it go
What is love?
I want to know

A Romantic Writer

I'm a lover
Not a fighter
I'm a romantic writer

Red rose petals
On the floor
She saw this
When she opened the front
door

Let me touch your body
In ways never touched before
My every move
Will have you yearning for more

Let me please you
Ease your tension
Let me put you in your favorite
sexual position

Every step I take
Every motion I make
I will keep you wet
Like a lake

I'm a thin dude
But I know how to do my thing
Love you the right way
I'll make your other lips sing

I'm a lover

I will love you in every way
Sexual healing from me
Will have you feeling okay

I know a lot
Variety
Expert in the bedroom
A great commodity

Just letting you know
Understand
I am a grown man

I'm a lover
Not a fighter
I'm a romantic writer

Girl You're Something Else

Lately I been thinking about
you
You're constantly on my mind
Girl you're something else
This means you're fine

Girl you're something else
This is what I say
When your lips touch my lips
My breath is taking away

I get lost in your kisses
This means when you kiss me I
lose control
You're the star in my movie
You have the lead role

Your seductive techniques
Are exciting and thrilling
Being with you
Gives me a great feeling

Ecstasy is what I'm
experiencing now
Damn, Wow I repeat
Your pleasure spot I love to eat
And position my tongue down
there
I enjoy squeezing your breasts
and messing up your hair

Lovely brown eyes and a cute
mole above your lips
I like touching your soft behind
and placing my hands on your
curvy hips

You make me blush
Whenever you stare at me
I like having you around
And there with me

I don't know where this is going
But I'm willing to travel in that
direction
And experience more of your
sensual and sexual affection

Just having you in my life
makes me smile
Girl you're my something else
I hope this relationship last for
a long while

Lately I been thinking about
you
You're constantly on my mind
Girl you're something else
This means you're fine

Smooth Criminal

I steal hearts
I'm a thief
A smooth criminal
Providing sexual relief

It feels like I've lived
Many lives
I've had more women
Than pharaoh had wives

Women
What can I say
I love them
In everyway

Various
Variety
Abundance
Plenty

One by one, Two by two
Three by three
The ladies
Can't get enough of me

Player
My description
I admit
I like pimping

I've learned from the best

I studied the greats
I confess
A lot of dates

She's sexy
She's fine
She belongs to me
She's mine

He thought he had her
He wasn't right
She's in my bed
Every night

I know her
Very well indeed
I just had to have her
I'm filled with greed

I steal hearts
I'm a thief
A smooth criminal
Providing sexual relief

Naked

I like the way you move
I like the way you shake it
But I really like it
When you're naked

I want to make love to you
once, twice
Again makes three
You make me say wee
Hooray
I can sex you all night and day

Naked
I can't wait for you to take it all
off
My hands on your clothing
I begin to take it all off

Your clothes
I remove
My lips placed on your skin
Made your body move

Your body
The way it look
Your lower region
Is the direction I took
That place I explore
I need it more and more

Sex

That's what I'm talking about
Listening to your pleasure
shout
I enjoy
Continue to evade
Deploy

Can I suck on your neck?
Can I taste your flavor?
You're fruity
I like this flavor

I'm going down
I'm traveling deep
Last night
We didn't sleep
Keep
Can I have it?
Your love is my addiction
I got to have it

I'm seductive
Seduction
Pretty soon climax
Climatic eruption

I like you bare
Like copy paper
I can't wait to put my ink on all
over her

I like the way you move
I like the way you shake it

But I really like it
When you're naked

Sexual Connection

Enjoying each other sexually
Sexual aggression
We have a bond
A sexual connection

I'm feeling emotions
Never felt before
I enjoy being with you
I want to experience more

Sexual
You're definitely are
You're still the best by far

I think about you often
You're on my mind right now as
I lay in bed
Fantasizing
I'm eager to sex you on my bed

Exploring each other
Discovering our space
Making love to you
Sends me to special place

You keep me fed
Fulfilled
Your love keeps my heart filled
With so much glee
Overwhelming
I'm experiencing hilarity

I'm inside of you
Feeling every motion
I'm going deep
I'm like a submarine in an
ocean

Whenever I spend time with
you
The more infatuated I be
You're so special to me

Meeting you was destiny
We had to meet
You're still my favorite meal
and treat

I love to eat
And devour you
I love it
When you let me overpower
you
And take over
I also enjoy it
When you overpower me and
take over

Enjoying each other sexually
Sexual aggression
We have a bond
A sexual connection

I'm a Sex Vet

I create moisture
I can make you wet
A professional lover
I'm a Sex Vet

I bet
I guarantee
You will receive total
satisfaction from me

I do whatever
Whenever
No one can love you better
Because I'm great
Eager for sex
I can't wait

Can I play with you?
Foreplay
Let me orally sex you as your
body lay

When I touch your spot
You get creamy like pudding-
Jello
Your delicious dessert
Makes me a mellow fellow

Down below
I'm tasting
I'm moisturizing you

Basting

I want to lick you where I stick
you
I want to stick you where I lick
you
Lets televise our sexual
activities
I want to porno flick you

Sex with me is a remedy
It can heal your broken heart
I told her this at the start
When we begin
She is my weekend friend

Friday and Saturday
The days we spend together
I'm a postman
I deliver in all types of weather

A variety of techniques
Seductive in every way
Women love Prince Jay
I make them all feel wonderful
and okay

I will love you
The way its intended
Just like Trey Songz
Sex I invented

I create moisture

I can make you wet
A professional lover
I'm a Sex Vet

I Have That Affect

A lot of attention
No neglect
Total fulfillment
I have that affect

I have that affect
I can make a woman wet
She let
Me in the front door
Later on that night she's telling
me *don't stop*
Give me more

Adore
The ladies want me
I'm so mysterious
They constantly ask who is he
Inquiring minds want to know
I'm exploring
Traveling below
Going down
Creating bedroom music
Sex sound

I have that affect
I give women joy
I have that affect
I obtain what they need to
create a girl or boy

I have that affect

I'm a heart healer
I can also excite your mind and
soul
I am a thriller

A lot of attention
No neglect
Total fulfillment
I have that affect

Red Alert

I'm a Casanova
Just like Gerald Levert
I'm on the prowl
Red alert

Red alert
I'm looking
So many women tooking
Taken
Sexual movements
I'm making
Motion
Bedroom filled with commotion
Noise
I know what I'm doing
I have unlimited poise

Red alert
Ring the alarm
I'm charismatic
This means I have unlimited
charm

She likes the Prince Jason
tattoo on my arm
And my pierced ear
I said, I like your body
Especially your rear
And of course your chest
But your pretty eyes and smile
I like those the best

She said, you're just trying to
get in my pants
I said, yeah that's true
But honestly
I really want to get to know you
Will you allow me to?

She's staring at me
I gave her a wink
She said, you have a dirty mind
Jason I know how you think

I said, ok
Now it's time to show you how I
feel
I slightly grinned
Displaying some of my sex
appeal

I'm a Casanova
Just like Gerald Levert
I'm on the prowl
Red alert

Poetic Playboy

Pleasing women
Every way I can
I'm a poetic playboy
Sexy man

I'm a poetic playboy
Women love my appearance
I asked her, Can I be with you?
She gave me clearance
She said, Yes you may
We also had sex that same day

I'm a poetic playboy
Using my words to meet women
My poetry helps me greet
women
I'm very sweet to women
They adore me
It's hard for them to ignore me
I have their attention
I'm a stress reliever
I eliminate their tension
Using my sexual healing
Having fun in the bedroom
Exciting and thrilling

I love women
Yes I truly do
I told her every time we make
love
It feels brand new

Pleasing women
Every way I can
I'm a poetic playboy
Sexy man

My Little Freak

A good time
Is what she seek
I'm enjoying her company
She's my little freak

Be my little freak
Make my knees buckle
She placed her hands on my belt
And unfastened my buckle

She removed my pants
Took a glance
She said, Damn Jason
You got a lot in your pants

Be my little freak
Give me something to sweet to eat
Before she had a boyfriend
Now he's obsolete
Delete
He doesn't exist anymore
My charisma overwhelmed her
She couldn't resist anymore

Up and down, Back and forth
Erotic friction
I have amazing stamina
Great condition

Attention
Be aware
She took all I had to offer
She accepted my dare

She told me to rock that thang
I deep cocked that thang
Climax
I after shocked that thang
She's experiencing a
pleasurable feel
She said, Boy you're the real
deal

My little freak
Get freaky
She said, I wasn't expecting
that from you
Jason you're sneaky

My little freak
She does whatever
I'm her favorite
Because I'm better
And different from all the rest
Sexually
I'm the best

My little freak
She's all over the place
She started down below
Now she's up on my face
Giving me a taste

She knows what I like
And I love her taste

My little freak
She's so fine
My little freak
She's all mine

She likes to drink wine
Red and white
A pair of handcuffs and a
blindfold
We used those items last night

Role-play
We do a lot together
I admit role-playing
Makes sex better
Exciting and fun
I have so many stories to tell
More and a ton

A good time
Is what she seek
I'm enjoying her company
She's my little freak

Down South

I know every spot
That makes a woman hot
Down south
I visit this place a lot

Remember my poem, **Visitation**
My invitation between her hips
I enjoy kissing those lips
In between
Right now I feel like a horny
teen

Orally, sexually
I know what to do
Multiple women at the same
time
Then there was two

If only you knew
I admit I'm a freak
A woman's pleasure
I always seek

I can't help it
I'm a Casanova man
Seducing ladies
Yes I can
Yes I will
Women enjoy my ride
They say it's a thrill

I know every spot
That makes a woman hot
Down south
I visit this place a lot

Night Shift

I give women a sexual boost
Uplift
I perform after hours
Night Shift

I'm like a vampire
I only come out at night
I enjoy sucking on a woman's
neck
And gently bite

When your man is not around
Call me and I'm on my way
A lot of sex games
We often play

A pleasurable start
And a satisfying end
Sneak out, sneak in
We hang out every weekend

I'm at my apartment lying in
bed
My cell phone ring
She said, Hey can you come
over?
My reply, Yeah sweet thing

Anything goes
She don't care

She said, Have a baby by me
baby be a millionaire
50 cent
Her vagina feels like its heaven
sent

Dominant
She loves to take control
I feel like I'm marijuana high
My eyes begin to roll
When she touch me the right
way
An oral experience as I lay

She calls me Hot Boy
Mr. Good Bar
She says, Freaky Jay
You're the best by far

My special techniques
No man can match
I win every time
Conquering each match
Sexual battle
I was good
She started to tattle
Couldn't keep it to herself
I was great
I'm proud of myself

I give women a sexual boost
Uplift
I perform after hours

Night Shift

Her Favorite Sex Toy

Just like Martin and Gina
She said, You go boy
She told me
I was her favorite sex toy

A lot of guys have their own
style
I'm telling you about mine
Whispering in her ear
Girl you're fine

Grab her behind
Softly squeeze
It's her turn now
She got on her knees

She's eager to please
I'm ready to enjoy
She pass my interview
It's time to employ

I'm a professional
I'm a pro
They call me a male ho
A Giggalo

She's screaming my name
I told her baby chill out
You're going to get me evicted
Or thrown out

She continues to shout
Screaming again
I'm making it wet
She's creaming again

Just like Martin and Gina
She said, You go boy
She told me
I was her favorite sex toy

Lights, Camera, Action

Fulfillment
Sexual satisfaction
We're making love
Lights, camera, action

Take your clothes off
Remove them slowly
She's looking at me sinfully
We're about to do something
unholy

She started at the top
Took off her brazier
She told me come here
Take off my underwear

I moved down below
I opened my mouth
Removed her panties with my
teeth
I love going south
Where her pleasure is located
Last nite I ate it
And tonite I'm gonna eat
It tastes good and sweet

A delicious treat
Number one dessert
She is enjoying herself
Going berserk

She's shaking her behind
A lot of booty movement
She's in her comfort zone
I see improvement
Comfortable doing something
new
I suggested lets bring in
another woman
Two
Me, you and she
She said okay
Now the total is three

So happy
This was my luck day
Unforgettable
It happened back in the day

Fulfillment
Sexual satisfaction
We're making love
Lights, camera, action

Zodiac

I'm a lover
A sex maniac
Informing you about some
women I knew
Zodiac

Sex with an Aries is aggressive
Adventurous
They're dominating, rough and
quick
Sex with an Aries is a little bit
dangerous

Sex with a Taurus is passionate
Lack of sexual variety
Old- fashioned type
Security and stability

Sex with a Gemini is full of
novelty and excitement
Trying anything and everything
nearly anywhere
Gemini women will do it
anywhere

Sex with a Cancer is a fully
encompassing sexual
experience
Lots of tender foreplay,
messages afterwards, candles
lit by the beside

Soft music in the background
Just sit back and enjoy the ride

Sex with a Leo is sensual
Affectionate
Scented oils, rubbing
Also passionate

Sex with a Virgo
It's straightforward and direct
No fancy moves, games or
place
This is what to expect

Sex with a Libra
It's an enchanting experience
Like a sex scene out of a movie
An amazing experience

Sex with a Scorpio is
passionate
Emotional
Intensity
Sex with a Scorpio is physical

Amazing stamina
Can last all night
Acting out sexual fantasies
Having sex with a Scorpio is all
right

Sex with a Sagittarius consist of
out door sex, one night stands

They like to explore
Anything goes
They will have you wanting
more

Sex with a Capricorn
In the bedroom, they will last
all night
And want some more
Good at what they do
They also will have you craving
for more

Sex with an Aquarius
Imaginative
They're fun and silly
Creative

Sex with a Pisces
Lots of seduction and role-play
Erotic games
And activities to play

I'm a lover
A sex maniac
Informing you about some
women I knew
Zodiac

My Story to Date...

Jason O'Neal Williams was born in Houston, Texas on July 21, 1978. He lived there for 8 years. He and his family later moved to Homer, Louisiana. He attended Homer High school and Grambling State University. Both schools are in Louisiana. He graduated from Homer High School in 1996 and Grambling State University on May 19, 2002 with a Bachelors of Science degree in marketing. At the tender age of 23, he began writing poetry. He started writing poetry in 2001 at a dark point in his life. He started writing poetry his last year in college. Before a recurring dream, he had no interest in poetry and didn't take any poetry classes. He recalled having the same dream night after night for three days straight. When he awoke from the first dream, he decided to write about it because it was so intense.

When he wrote about the dream, it came out in a rhyme. He didn't pay any attention to the dream or poem because he thought it was a fluke or mistake. The next night, same dream another and different rhyme. The next night, same dream another and different rhyme. He kept having the same dream with different points of views about it. His response to those dreams was poetry. That dream changed and saved his life. Before the dream he was frustrated, depressed, and stressed out. He was ready to give up on himself and life. He was very suicidal. After that experience, he knew something special was happening to him. This was something that he could avoid or ignore.

At first he was afraid of this talent. He didn't understand what was happening to him. Because waking one day with a talent that you never had before can scare anyone. With a little more time and his faith in God, he finally understood and accepted it.

From that moment on, he was never the same. He became another person, "The Prince of Poetry". He has the ability to change the world and make a difference. And he fully accepts the responsibility that he has. God gave him this gift to help him deal with life. God gave him this gift to help others as well. God gave him this gift at the time he needed it.

On March 2002, he attended and competed at the International Poetry convention in Orlando, Florida. The convention was held at the world famous Disney Coronado Springs Resort, located in Walt Disney World. The convention included workshops, seminars, readings, rap sessions, poetry contests and poetry critiques. It was a great experience for him.

He learned a lot about his craft. It was basically three days of non-stop poetry and entertainment. He had the chance to meet different poets from all over the world. He didn't win the poetry competition but it didn't discourage him. It just boosted his determination and drive to be the best poet he could be. That day he promised himself that he was not going to let anything or anyone stand in his way from becoming a poet and a published author.

Also in 2002, he was nominated for International Poet of the year and received the 2002 International Poet of Merit award. He also received the 2002 Editor's choice award for his poem "I Want To Succeed". He also has 3 poems published in other poetry anthologies, Silent Solitude (2002), New Millennium Poets (2002) and 2004 International Who's Who In Poetry (2004). He was the only American featured poet for that year.

In 2003 at the age of 24, he made his debut as an author with his first book of poetry called "My Story, Through My

Eyes". This book is based on his life. It's about his experiences, thoughts and feelings. It was published by Publish America. Mr. Williams has done a lot in such a short time. His 2nd book of poetry called, "E.3" (Experiencing Death, Emotional Disturbance, Everlasting Love) was published May 2004.

This book was also published by Publish America. This book is the sequel to "My Story, Through My Eyes." It is the continuation of the story. It's about life, his life, and the life of others. This book is more personal. It shows his maturity and vulnerability as a person, poet and writer. This book is filled with unbelievable emotion.

Prince Jason O'Neal Williams is a talented person, poet, and writer. He is a young man with a special gift. He has a gift that others can benefit from. He has the ability to change, inspire, encourage, or influence. He has the potential of becoming great someday. This is only the beginning for him. There's a lot more to come in the future.

Author's Accomplishments

Jason O'Neal Williams

"Prince Jason"

The Prince of Poetry

- 2002 International Poet Of The Year nominee
- 2002 International Poet Of Merit Award
- January 2002 Editor's Choice Award
- 2002 Inductee of The International Society of Poets
- First appearance in Ebony magazine (November 2003 issue) on page 201.
- 2003 Member of the Writers' League of Texas (Austin, Texas)
- 2004 Pinkie Carolyn Wilkerson award for poetry-presented by Grambling State University
- 2004 International Who's Who In Poetry-The only American featured poet for that year

- 2006 Pinkie Carolyn Wilkerson award for poetry-presented by Grambling State University
- 2006 Poetry writer for Black College Today Magazine
- 2008 Poetry Editor for Starving Writers Publishing
- 2008 appearance in the movie Harold and Kumar 2

5917699R0

Made in the USA
Charleston, SC
20 August 2010